MW01088613

9 25
4 95

THE NATIONAL POETRY SERIES

The National Poetry Series was established in 1978 to publish
five collections of poetry annually through five participating
publishers. The manuscripts are selected by five poets of
national reputation. Publication is funded by James A. Michener,
Edward J. Piszek, The Ford Foundation, The Witter Bynner
Foundation, and the five publishers—Doubleday, E. P. Dutton,
Harper & Row, Random House, and Holt, Rinehart & Winston.

The National Poetry Series—1981

George Barlow, GUMBO *(Selected by Ishmael Reed)*
Larry Levis, THE DOLLMAKER'S GHOST *(Selected by Stanley Kunitz)*
Robert Peterson, LEAVING TAOS *(Selected by Carolyn Kizer)*
Michael Ryan, IN WINTER *(Selected by Louise Glück)*
Reg Saner, SO THIS IS THE MAP *(Selected by Derek Walcott)*

Books by Robert Peterson

Home for the Night
The Binnacle
Wondering Where You Are
Under Sealed Orders
Lone Rider
Leaving Taos

Robert Peterson

LEAVING TAOS

Selected by Carolyn Kizer

1817

HARPER & ROW, PUBLISHERS, New York
Cambridge, Hagerstown, Philadelphia, San Francisco,
London, Mexico City, São Paulo, Sydney

for Ken, and Leonard,
and Gina

The excerpt from *Light Years* by James Salter, is reprinted by permission of the author.

Some of these poems originally appeared in *Home for the Night* (Kayak), *The Binnacle* (Lillabulero), *Wondering Where You Are* (Kayak), *Under Sealed Orders* (Cloud Marauder), and *Lone Rider* (Dingo).
Grateful acknowledgment is made to the editors of the following magazines for permission to reprint: "Leaving Taos" first appeared in *Kayak;* "Moonglow, High Clouds, New Snow" in *Crow Call;* "Nacho Jimenez (Stockton) vs. Richie Manchaca (Pittsburg)" and "Sparrow" in *Quarry West;* and "Thinking About What to Do Next" in *New Letters.*

FIRST EDITION

Designer: Sidney Feinberg

Library of Congress Cataloging in Publication Data

Peterson, Robert, 1924 (June 2) –
    Leaving Taos.

    (The National poetry series)
    I. Kizer, Carolyn. II. Title III. Series:
National poetry series.
PS3566.E7712L4 1981   811'.54   80–8693
ISBN 0–06–014839–X
ISBN 0–06–090875–0 (pbk.)

81 82 83 84 85 10 9 8 7 6 5 4 3 2 1

Contents

GERMANY 1945

EVENING POEMS

There is no complete life. There are only fragments. We are born to have nothing, to have it pour through our hands. And yet, this pouring, this flood of encounters, struggles, dreams . . . one must be unthinking, like a tortoise.

JAMES SALTER, Light Years

Preface

Robert Peterson is that rare possessor of a faultless ear for the rhythms of contemporary speech, both city and country; in a phrase of Kenneth Hanson's (another fine, elegant poet who deserves to be better known), "he always gets the set of the words just right." But Peterson has suffered the handicap of being a citizen of the West, where poets are supposed to have loud voices and marketable eccentricities. One might call him a "lieder poet"; with his wonderfully tuned, perfectly trained vocal apparatus, he is able to do almost anything with it except scream. He has learned a good deal from Pound—his letters as well as his poetry. Much of his work is carefully colloquial, written in pure American into which traces of literary reference—East and West—are gently blended. I frequently find Peterson's simplest statements curiously moving: "The yellow cat has gone to see the white cat"—in its setting, a kind of domestic pastoral. Here is the whole "Evening Poem":

> Enlightenment should come easily
> noting the absence of wind.
>
> But it's a measuring worm
> on an ivy leaf
> that attracts attention.
>
> The yellow cat has gone to see the white cat.
> Petals of four kinds of camellia
> fall gracefully into sadness
>
> And there is nothing to improve
> the extravagant silence.
>
> Flowing through silk sleeves
> are all memories
> of previous things.
>
> And the pine tree beyond the garden
> is seen again
> to be a resting place

> For birds
> who come no nearer.

Or take the last stanza of one of his best-known poems, "Jean Gabin as Ship":

> But what he thinks isn't important.
> It's that smooth, well-trimmed walk
> between the big scenes
> I go to see. Try it myself
> sometimes, when I've a need
> to be making not love but speed
> with lots of deep water under me.

A strong, brave male poet friend of mine was reading this aloud when, much to his consternation, he burst into sobs. Perhaps it's that combination of the marvelously balanced line with a touch of nostalgia for the unlived life (catalyzed by our emotions about great old films and great old actors). It is not coincidental that it was another poet to be so moved: a member of, alas, the all-too-exclusive fellowship of Peterson's admirers. We sit around too late at night, and sigh over lines like:

> Growing older, I seem to drink less.
> And good and bad intentions cling together like wet leaves.

Perhaps you've had to try to achieve this effect, many and many a time, to feel the full measure of pleasure when another poet succeeds. But one hopes that with the publication of this book by a distinguished house, these smiles, these tears, these durable pleasures will be shared by a wider audience.

CAROLYN KIZER

IN THAT PART OF THE CITY

(Sonnets)

A Freezing Night on Cambridge Common

A freezing night on Cambridge Common
beneath the tree
where Washington
took command of the Troops

Feet in rags
one of the Continental Corporals
I come to Attention

But why am I not in bed
with a woman
or a mystery
in a warm room?

Why am I not the tree?
Why not Zeus?

Why not Washington?

You've Been Sent Off

You've been sent off in the rain
to walk in the city
while I remain here in my country chair
memorizing a bit of Baudelaire.

Hoping that your troubles
will lose you there.
Who knows
what else?

When I'm feeling restless
I usually hit the bottle
where all kinds of illusions

Can be stood on their heads
and one crazy move wins the game.
But it takes practice.

Hands Folded Like Napkins

Hands folded like napkins in my lap
I'm staring willfully at the future.
Just one of the crowd, a bystander.
It's my teeth they're after.

Someone's trimming a hedge,
the Paris Express arrives. . . .
It's the last lap at Le Mans, and the band is playing.
What's the sound of one castanet, decaying?

Across my nose, Doctor and Nurse speak in code:
"Are we cementing Mrs. Kershman's crown?"
"What became of Fred?" "I'm going on a diet."

I can't nod. Even my beard is Novocained.
Just concentrate on letting normal thoughts flow naturally.
She's built. Does she or doesn't she?

The Second Year

The second year, two rhododendrons bloomed.
The petals fell one by one
and were placed on water—a splash of pink
in the south room.

Red geraniums also, making few demands.
And nomadic nasturtiums found their own way.
Among the usual weeds
a primrose was carefully guided.

The second year the deer, returning
enjoyed each and every dahlia bud, and I said
all redwoods are true.

But contained in their beauty only, the rhododendrons
came and went like lovers.
And won't be seen again.

In the 2 A.M. Club

In the 2 A.M. Club, a blue-collar bar,
waiting for a suit to be pressed
a desire to review all human emotions
is inspired by three beers.

Clever the sun, seen through cold bourbon highballs.
Eternally undismayed are the pool shooters.
And greed is discovered in a sack of peanuts,
not what it was a year ago.

The fear of being alone
can be eased
by thoughts of switches.

I'm surrounded by unknown men
and my life to this moment
can't be totally explained.

We're Sitting Around a Table

We're sitting around a table
beneath a yellow umbrella on a bright afternoon
celebrating the little boy's birthday.
He got a bicycle.

His older sister's angry; he's being spoiled.
He also got a secret service radio and a racetrack.
This is a comedy.
Isn't the garden beautiful?

We're drinking gin.
Wildflowers, films, carved ivory, and blood poisoning
are discussed honestly.

A whistle blows. It's five o'clock! The children
have gone.
We're drunk but not noisy.
How many of us *are* there?

On My Birthday

On my birthday
I visit Hanson
who by the way he moves without seeming to move
honors both silence and Confucius.

"To consume beer steadily by the hour
is to grow older like the shadows
of birds," he says. "And one does not need to know
German to translate German,

one simply works backwards."

We drink to the original Invisible Man,
who's just died of stomach trouble.
And ponder the fate of poets in an age of prose.

My brain is a boulevard, peopled with stylish words.
His cigar smoulders like an inactive volcano.

A Swim in Ohuira Bay

A swim in Ohuira Bay:
ten strokes from pier to float,
twenty back.
Here the self is naked and wet;

In this current
strategists and dreamers drown.
Keep one eye on Mexico
or forget it.

Water green as trees
and warm as bread,
fish rising to feed, all sorrows

At kissing level.
And overhead wild ducks soar like tracers
into forms as delicious as life or money.

Mazatlán

Mazatlán—an open system
of forgetfulness and slow clocks.
No news. Every day turns to dinner
and lunch is becalmed in bananas.

I burn on the beach. Or I'm blue
and weep without shame under palms
for the Welsh
or old postponements.

A world is crumbling by the hour.
The mosquitoes are living on their nerves.
Why bother fish?

The list of things I'll not do
grows comfortably long. And on the Gulf
sunsets create themselves for me
like exquisite things that have already happened.

I'm Walking to the Bay

I'm walking to the bay, a mile to go.
A nymph poses in a window.
There's haze and smoke over Richmond.
I take the hills easy and slow.

It's teatime, and I'm meditating on the grass.
A poodle recovers from an obedience test.
My thorax is flooded with intelligence.
Familiar things are happening in the bars on Sansome Street.

Pvt. Joseph Merrell passes Alcatraz, outbound
for Saigon with carbine ammunition, morphine
and replacements, 10,000 miles to go

And the homeward commuters from Dago to Seattle
speed by in all makes and models
wondering who loves them.

Athens

Athens: a bloodshot sunset.
Choir practice begins next door to the bakery.
Soda pop is mixed with wine. And those loud explosions
can only mean the Queen is having her baby.

This is the life! It's not my job
to describe beautiful caves. A drowsy gypsy
is the breeze, personified. And you, tonight
Oahu carnations.

At 3 A.M., a sleek whore in *Le Roi* smacks her gums.
Tourists drift by like dubious zebras.
Diesel Germans are still counting the stones.

The lion is long-gone,
there's nothing but moonshine
But let's make love anyway.

The Yellow Cat

The yellow cat speeds down the hall at midnight;
another mouse dished up to oblivion.
The house creaks.
It has its own problems.

Raised to be a surgeon
I've lived a life of dreams and crime.
Poems and cookies are all we can offer
if your parents come.

Will sober thoughts
in the morning
make me lovable?

Growing older, I seem to drink less.
And good and bad intentions cling together like wet leaves.
Not even the passage of time is perfect.

The Bird

The bird
weighs less than a dollar
on my palm.

Spread one wing with a finger
to make a miniature fan.
Silk throat the color of yolk.

And if I close the hand
Presto! it's gone.

Bodies of mice drop from sight
into brambles
farther down,

flipped by their tails.

But a bird—no leverage.
I whisper once on its feathers to see my breath.

The Dog Is Breaking Down

The dog is breaking down.
To and fro he runs around the clock, pissing on seedlings
and chasing moths and butterflies
into the house.

He can't think. Sticks worry him. He'll eat
six biscuits in a row, then bark at the box.
His owners don't know, they think he's fearless.

But he's a loser.
Dreams of unnatural relationships,
and blinks, cow-eyed,
when sparrows perch on his nose.

Loved only by his fleas, as doomed
as we are

He's trying to keep busy.
But his nerves are shot. He'll be killed by a car.

Famous for Comfort

for Leonard Gardner

Famous for Comfort was the Fielding ad.

And the bellboys were men:
Tom was kept by a Canadian gypsy,
Frank made it with a moustache.
Red taught me trays and keys
and the tips in laundry and ice.
When Bill, a tenor, was late
we dialed the Turkish Baths.

Ralph planned to be a bookie, and was nice to stiffs.
Harry loved stud, and was in hock to his curls.
Sid had a limp, a gun, and three girls.

Flush with cash, they went off to Reno
to drink in hotels, and lose at Keno,

Dreaming of the spiritual life in Florida.

Now and Then

Now and then I find myself
in that part of the city
where I used to live
when I was young.

So many things have happened since I left.
So much changed.
And the few people I still know
don't recognize me.

I look up at the window that used to be mine
in days when my father owned the hotel.
And remember, before going on

How as a widower he played poker with Hughey and Sven,
knew the Mayor, and insisted that someday
I'd be President of the Association.

LEAVING TAOS

Dusk, Zone 1

Fish not biting.
My 40¢ farm worms starving.

Just two swallows
surgeons of the soul

Making business calls.

Loon Lake
knows it all

But I'm new here.

Summer Evening, Ranchos

Leaning on a porch post.
Soft line of willows beyond my glass, & beyond them
one more sun going down.

The cat floats out, & back in. A possible sign
something's been forgiven.

Apple light on troubled clouds: soft-spoken
but not to be believed. Still, it could be coming
in a strange tongue
from the right place.

Over the power line, a hundred swifts
hurrahing through that cathedral of air
like a convention
of tossed silk hats.

Another night on the land.
In the best sense, they come & go for nothing.
Vino Fino the wine. Everything else happening
down the road.

Lone Rider

An old bitch, abandoned
once called Chester
missing front leg
& what looks like a bullet wound
over one eye
who shags over, cold-nosed
odd days around sundown
to sniff what's new
& pretend to suffer
a few affections
not knowing our names
& owned by no one
in particular

No barks or howls. We offer bones
& biscuits. Stays an hour, maybe
then slips through our hands
down the Mora road
until next time
for our purposes

Taos dog
it's late October
& she's gone

To Truchas

Climbing steep trail with wet feet
trying so hard
to be happy
I could get pneumonia. . . .

Resting in rain
on a knee of the mountain
thoughts traveling
in four simple directions

My brain
a flying horse
whose eyes look down
on quiet, brief lives.

Autumn

Pickpocket leaves/the wind
in its borrowed overcoat . . .

Two crows
like black eyebrows

On the stubborn face
of a sky

Sonnet for Grandpa

Some bourbon with my landlord—the old man.
80 last week, & we're kicking that around.
He's cooking chicken. His cat is George.
The shortwave's tuned to Poland.

His only son, 50, the doctor, collects kimonos.
Now & then runs outside aiming a .30-30
at the Sangre de Cristos, some faithless guy, or the stars.
His knees knock. His money talks. The Sheriff comes & goes.

Time passes; we switch to South Africa. He sighs
for Junior, damns the local law, we look over a gas bill.
Gay life is kid-stuff. And Scotch drinkers must be crazy.

I confess to awe of 80. "Shit," he says. "You don't get
wise, and you never get well. Just a bit owled
and overtaken once in a while."

Skunk

Night-caught in Maestas' corn.
Moves, sometimes he moves
& the trap moves. Then nothing but clouds
for a long time.

None of my business, no.
But he won't kill it. Something to do with
being hit twice in one year
by lightning. He'll wait.

Get the pistol close, close enough
to be clean, & let it in. . . .
Wild one, corn-thief, sufferer—whatever,
right to the end
quiet that long time.

Now I'm walking away.
Never knew that fur was so tough.
You could use it for fences.

Polecat, friend, you go
& I stay.

Sparrow

Let it rest on my hand a moment in the sun
like a warm leaf cooled by late summer rain.

Then fold the fingers lightly in, & as one
for no reason hurls a convenient stone

Fling it, blind, beyond the trees, into the wind
as far as I can.

A passing regret, a silent turn, a minor grief.

       Look away from these,
       let them end

       Before this small death
       comes to earth

       Among my neighbor's plums & mint.

November

Last leaves, taking new shapes
say goodbye to the bough.
Raccoons float through the night
like warm bundles. A troubled friend
wanders.

(White are the old landmarks, blue-green
the best seas . . .)

In the East
scatterings of sparrows
fall on the first snow
watched by owls.

By his fire the cat
lost in a dream of diamonds, skillfully pretends
he's completely alone.

January of This Year

for Michael Parrish

1

Barometer falling. And who can prove on any given day
that a man isn't one year older than he was the same day
last year?

Schlitz & Beam. Beam & Schlitz. Watching first snowflakes
begin to smooth over
all the rough edges.

Do I speak the Spanish? An academic question. The man
in the mirror: definitely Cortez, slightly out of focus
at 47.

2

Believe me, it was dark out there. And I'm not sorry
you worried. Just keep in mind
this is my first blizzard.

Dinner watching *Show Boat.*
You laughed when I sang "Old Man River." But I knew
what I was doing. We've got to close ranks & keep rolling.

Clear today, & down to Zero. Once more, it comes to
looking for one real pearl in a timeless ton of snow
with a borrowed shovel.

Even the threads can hang by a thread.

Cracking Its Drunken Bones

Cracking its drunken bones, a storm
spits at the windows.
And the fat creek
is a noisy congratulation.

Sleeping badly, I become in dreams
more sensitive. But year after year
my barber keeps silent.
We're both smokers who need friends.

No one
this half of the century
is either young or old:

Tragic actors of the time
peering through pitiful trees
just for the hell of it.

Herbs, Flowers, Fruits & Things

for Lelli

Yes to ivy
in rain, & blue

The unborn carnation generation
& routine geraniums

Crocus, belladonna, henbane
& the grass, obviously

Thrust of the thistle
bonsai lentissimo

And the apple
being done unto

Fir, cedar, oak & pine
& myrtle for you

Magnolia I can say all day
but not orchid

And gardenias
taketh away

Call the woman I'd have
a little orange tree

That goes walking, my dog
Sigmund A. T. Freud (A

For acorn, T for
tangerine)

And me,
Nutmeg

Moonglow, High Clouds, New Snow

Unspoken light
on the commonplace things
of the world

Deaf hills & careworn fields
at the poor end of town

The long-legged hound
haloed in her one & only house

All part of a dream in off-white:
ten thousand nights

Of silence, weariness
and sanity.

The Young Conquistador

The young conquistador arrives at odd hours
without an appointment. Strikes piratical poses.
Demands spice, opium, salve, banknotes
& liqueurs.

Or displays lurid chapters of his life
written in green ink
on torn pages of his clothes.
We speak of naked nymphs & huge sums of gold.

I suggest he throw out his good suits
& alibis, pedal south in the off-season
to study ancient games of the Aztecs.

But he's not keen on sports
& his bicycle's falling apart. His mother's
last hope: that he'll give up vice for art.

Complaint #2

Whatever happened to Raffles, Moriarty, Willie Sutton?
Too many crooks these days, no brains, no class.
No wonder they're phasing out the Foreign Legion.

The past, an ill-fitting hand-me-down.
Future, thin beer, bad credit, & more hustlers
in cheap flags & business suits.
Jimmy the Greek not even Greek?
                                    It's possible.

Once, back in the great nation, I drank to current events.
Now, sad-toothed & over-sober, I ponder sweat glands & cobras
while the President limps through Minsk.

New snow on the apple boughs: a bit of fresh hope?
Can the Living Mountain really become a great white sail?

Even the best-fed & well-loved dogs
are taking to the hills, arguing.

Camden, Six Foot Seven

Five wives ago
I watched this peanut
chasing soap bubbles
through the prune orchard.

His older brother
could balance him
by the thumbs, & his mother
couldn't stop apologizing.

Now this picture
in the *Gazette*
of an Alaskan oil prospector
holding a bronco bride

In one hand
& a Volkswagen
in the other, his beard
a herd of buffalo.

They'll honeymoon in Marrakech.

What goes on here?
What did he eat?
How does he vote?
Why didn't he write?

Winter Evening, Ranchos

A cold cow in a field counts off another day.
And a lone raven crosses the first star
like a dream of suicide.

Quilted in new snow, I freeze with the sheep.
A mean cur barks my way in broken circles.
We're both nowhere.

But part of the moon is
for a moment, all mine.
And a warm horse, close enough to touch.

Cabrezo Creek runs on to eternal satisfaction.
And the last shadows fold into the mountain
like felt obligations.

Happy Birthday

for Pat Robertson

A small February snow.
Overnight about enough
to cover a tomcat's paw.
My roof leaks in 13 places.

I'm bitching too
about a friend out West
who lives on a little hill
he calls a mountain.

Instead of complaining
in writing
you'd go straight there & ask him directly
who in hell he thinks he is.

Back here, my architect forgot to make a door
for the bathroom.
In this case I don't know what you'd do:
Tarot the culprit, put up a curtain, or buy a chisel?

You're the water-bearer, seeker of truth.
I'm one of those nervous June messengers.
Your sign has Lindbergh, Dr. Talley, & Clark Gable.
I've got Frank Lloyd Wright & Sartre.

Well, we won the war. Time to start drinking.
This wish has no words, but keep listening.
It's snowing again—just like a woman.
And I'm going downtown for more information.

The St. James Hotel

(Cimarron, N.M.)

Altogether, 26 men shot dead here.
And a Ute Chief whacked down just outside
by a white man
with a meat cleaver.

There must've been a few suicides too,
some routine disappearances,
bloody drunks puffing cheroots, in boots
& plenty of venery.

Down from Denver, I'm stopping over.
Tomorrow, stagecoach up the canyon
to Eagle's Nest
& Red River.

A pearl-handled theatrical producer
who later
under an alias
will discover gold
in Questa.

Snug in my vest, wax-moustached
& with 20/20 vision
I pinch a hostess, twirl a bourbon
& practice my Apache

as Kit Carson floats a check
& Pat Garrett cheats at stud.

Leaving Taos

for Marianna

Coming down from the fabled mountains
& back to a real city after some bad years,
it won't last but Albuquerque, N.M., seems like Paris
in its best days.

Once again I'm sitting in cafés on Rue de la Paix
free of former wives, winter fevers, & most sunsets.

I have returned everything, down to the last tack
ever borrowed in the wilderness from man or beast.

Paid every bill, made peace with the gods of morbid seasons
& oiled & stored all my pistols, secure in the knowledge
I'll never be missed by a single magpie or Indian.

Made my final comments on the Taos landscape—
                              or any landscape
for behold, I was not comforted by landscapes.

Once again I'm sitting in a baseball park on Sunday afternoon
after long years of meditations in canyons & gorges
which were sometimes called by other names
overcome by a flood of profound visual perceptions
which relate directly
to why my team is losing.

And the loons on Railroad Avenue smile knowingly
as I march east & west daily
to no place in particular
like a Dutch sailor.

A ruthless gang of red ants as big as backhoes
in the sugar—& other urban insects, but even so
                              have I come down

from the mad dogs, & *moradas,* & solitary soap operas
to resume building my cockeyed character
on the sidewalks & in the saloons
of Western civilization.

Looking for a woman who understands Rodin, Caruso
& earned-run averages
& can learn to fly a DC-10 in 6 days, if she has to.

GERMANY 1945

Le Havre

"By now
  you've probably arrived
  on foreign soil," she writes.

          Well
          at least I know
          who I am

Whose mother
but mine
would say that?

Doudeville

Smith & me
went off
to fuck Gilberte.

        But met

at gate
of the farm
by *le père*—

        Gives
        me & Smith

a jug
of calvados
to go away.

        Guzzling

under French moon
what a pair of
assassins!

He tried it again alone

        got eggs

Cologne

Front line:

B Co. in a mansion
Aid Station in a mansion
Everybody in a mansion, Rhine wine

                for everybody.

Some nuts
volunteer
for night patrols.

"Dear Mother, we're holding territory
in a quiet sector."

Souvenir pistols. Drunken passwords. German

                personal effects.

Scobey dances. I pop a boil.

                Now & then

a flare

Ruhr Pocket

Attacking north 5th day:

"Men, on your feet. Roosevelt's dead."

That night

a tree burst
wipes out
the Bridge Club.

"They got Smitty
in a straitjacket. He sez
he's in love."

Dry heaves

gray prisoners
gray smoke
gray civilians

goddam rain

"Lieutenant, I'm too tired."
"So am I. So am I."

"Where's the General?"
"I sure could use a good fuck."

My first beard

Clothes

caked
with nine men's blood

Ansbach

I listened to the guns
and shook

while Scobey bled
simply blinking swiftly

at the leaves
as if only

shocked
that the shell

should throw
his glasses   and his steel

up
to the sun

leave him   lightheaded

running   breathless
among   the aspens

Ingolstadt

House to house.

A whole squad
takes one
garage, blind
on champagne

        "Suppose
we get kicked back, who's going
to defend *me?*"

                (drowned
                in artillery)

Set on the south bank, heaving
at dawn
by the Engineers

"The Danube ain't blue.
Write that down, doc."

"342 made this mess. Them dead
is theirs."

"See that tank, men?
Your battle-wise ass
belongs to Patton."

    Where?

V–E Day Plus One

Hot food 35 pancakes

White flags
Bavarian beer
P-38's & Lügers

"Call me Wally," says the Captain.
"Didja know I'm a singer?"

"Colonel Boom-Boom got a medal."

"So this is the merry month of May."
"Where's the rabbi?"

                        Jesus Christ, I'm 21

& two
blue eyes

            all that bayonet drill
wasted

"What's the name of this place?"

Schlafen

EVENING POEMS

Baseball

In the last pocket of a threadbare afternoon
I found a park some boys,
five on one side
seven on the other,
were having Baseball
homeplate on a hill,
firstbase an imaginary place
everyone knew where was,
and out beyond
a real pond ducks sailed on.

The sides called
Come on and play Ump
and catcher-for-bothsides,
So I came on and we had
Baseball
for a long long time
until nobody remembered the score,
until we were only Three
against Two, six
shadows tilting under one evening star. . . .

Thinking About What to Do Next

No cheap thrills.

And no tennis. These two lovely young things
from rich families, for instance: obviously
plenty of expensive instruction
& play very well indeed. When they make mistakes

get mad at themselves & have tiny tennis tantrums.

But I'm the only spectator. Could these be for my benefit?

Nor will I stand in line
behind women with humdrum ankles
waiting to view Great Art Treasures. Or gaze into
difficult distances
heartlessly.

In the park the other day, a guy all alone in a green glade
in judo pajamas
practicing karate sequences: a white rose petal
of pure ambition.

And old men bowling on the green: concentrating
like comradely kings.

I ask a cop directions. First time I've ever talked
to Law, stoned, voluntarily.

Here's to the wine, butter, & cablegrams
of romance

the silence of swans

& what I've not yet spoken.

Beach at Cronkhite

One northbound freighter at five
is a good sign.

And one long wave, ending
can make a dream of aimless flight
turn wise

Against the land
that lets the freighter pass.

Distance takes its own light
from an eye
while I track pelicans home

As if trails of sand and time
were as much theirs
as motion

And this whole sea.

A Story

The note asking for locks & tokens was signed "a fair maiden."
You addressed me as Archie Moore, said I reminded you
of Memorial Day rodeos.

You seemed to belong to a season
of the last snows. I thought of spring water in tin cups,
Hannibal, & the sophisticated sounds of Linotype machines.

We agreed to meet the first day of sun & wind.
You dyed all your scarves to match my cowboy hat
stained with the sweat of rope tricks & whale watching;

Cleaned your canary, who renewed his membership.
Relived your arboreal life, rushed to the roof
crying "Eisenstein!"

Meanwhile the war went on though some of the wounded
recovered. But the day finally came. We met as planned
beneath my great painting *Philadelphia*.

What to do? Built a boat, which sold like a hotcake.
Then a bed. But preferred to sleep on our leaflets; became
overnight revolutionaries & organized debates.

Where did we want to go? But that was impossible.
The pyramids had not yet been built.
Nor had passports been invented.

Our urges multiplied, but conversation languished.
Even in your Sleeping Princess wardrobe you were bored.
So renounced garments. The bird flew listlessly through them.

Time came on. Some thieves were apprehended, rapists
sent to therapy, two Senators decayed, & a famous battleship
was surprised in shallow water.

Philadelphia was founded, Rome burned, Archie Moore
went to Australia, Rome was rebuilt,
Captain Bligh became Charles Laughton.

We discovered an Alp without a name. You wove a rug
the shape & color of your shadow in love
cast by hobo candles against the glacier

While I exercised in the volcano
with window sash weights said to have been found
in medieval outhouses.

The dawns passed through us like dull swords.
We spoke of constitutional law & camel-riding, & love
in the eyes of a dying sea turtle.

An umpire arrived with a decipherable message from Houdini.
The ice melted as we polished our chains.
A pterodactyl nested in the web that bound us.

But a day came when I found you in the meadow
seeming not to belong to a season of the last snows,
an alibi no one could accept.

Now I'm back in the hatband.
And you have your cathedral, & wild horses forever.
This is your map of the treasure.

Beside the Icebox

for Claude

Yesterday with first wife: brandy
in a dockside bar, switching on old lights,
looking out late
at our lives, talking

of Albair, her crazy stepfather
who wants to go back to France
on a motorcycle, & my odd aunt
who thinks I have a permanent cold.

Told her about you. She liked the sound
of your name—the way I said it. And left
at nine—off to a yoga lesson.

We split the check & I came home
& worried: where will *I* be
in the next life? Called you then

To explain where I'd been, but you
wouldn't talk—worried about me too.
Now dear, listen—this morning I've
polished some spoons, put two new

Avocado seeds to soak, I'm looking for you.
I've got a trick bird, & a box
of Evenings at Home incense. Do you
love me, still? I promise never to mention

you know again.

Sometimes, Besieged, I Forget How to Do It

When I forget how to do it
I've trouble conceiving trees, your eyes
are lost in leopards
& I watch myself closely, like a good leg
while Hamlet fences.

Soft as ashes, I invite bitches
to my rooms, light candles
& appeal to their decency,
but the thin-shinned Man
slides also in
& suddenly it's to be alone again,
a cold egg.

Off to the movies then, uncollected
to admire this genial, pearly Samurai
who lives on raw peas & gin
& has only to sneeze to know
Mercy is to know but not care
what any opponent, even a motorcycle, means.

To Myself, Late, in a Myrtle Grove

Outside my cheap candle
festive lights & log-truck rumble
distant, loaded, nearer
booming down the canyon
solid as a boulder.

Steak & fries
seasoned with fingers
fresh from fish.

Bed scooped with a foot.
No moon. Beer to the stars;
to the ladies

Of Coquille, Oregon
for this honest place
strong as a picnic table.

The night dark, close, & safe.
A clean river still running

And cows awake.

A Beauty

for Tally

Miss World of 19___
appearing in ballrooms
all over Europe
& the United Kingdom

Then leaving behind
your Copacabaña chorus turbans
& eyelashes
to tryst & tan
on Caribbean islands
with that ex-heavyweight millionaire counterspy

Now on-again, off-again
in a poor machismo town in your neat denims
with this unpronounceable Greek innkeeper
in hock to his ancient mother
no less than platonic debts
& oracular bachelorhood

Willowy, well-mannered
model of self-control, deep-south decorum
& long abstinence

Your only true loves privacy, one insatiable cat
& those old alcoholics
Brando & Quinn
lazy, heavy-lidded & mean
twirling violet toothpicks
as you light your own menthol cigars
unaffected by that lemony perfume on your chiffon scarves

Remember that time we discussed
the subtle fluttering of fans
even though you don't own a fan

& you said Paul Newman with a southern accent
your perfect teeth
& my sexy, unshaven shadow
just might combine
to transform the last vestige of loneliness
into an imperishable peach orchard?

Evening Poem

for Carolyn Kizer

Enlightenment should come easily
noting the absence of wind.

But it's a measuring worm
on an ivy leaf
that attracts attention.

The yellow cat has gone to see the white cat.
Petals of four kinds of camellia
fall gracefully into sadness

And there is nothing to improve
the extravagant silence.

Flowing through silk sleeves
are all memories
of previous things.

And the pine tree beyond the garden
is seen again
to be a resting place

For birds
who come no nearer.

Jean Gabin as Ship

In this plot he's a chef, falls
for his stepdaughter, loses
his best friend for it, etc.

There's some killing, things
finally get resolved, & he
comes back alone to his kitchen,
sadder, at the end.

But what he thinks isn't important.
It's that smooth, well-trimmed walk
between the big scenes
I go to see. Try it myself
sometimes, when I've a need
to be making not love but speed
with lots of deep water under me.

Outward Bound

(S.S. *Zvir*)

In this place, flags are coming down.
The last hatch clangs shut.
Brooklyn dockers joke & argue home.

Engines on. Listing some to Port at Half. As always,
gulls billowing aft.

Shore & harbor lights.
A Panama tramp at anchor off Jersey.
Overhead, a bridge called Verrazano.

Cargo, rags & heavy machinery for Yugoslavia.
People, ex-military from Texas & Florida
& their pokey wives, Dubrovnik & back.

The stars are O.K. They've got to belong there.
But the sea's something else. Taking itself too seriously
all the time

like the close friend
of a famous detective.

Rolling into a full gale.
The bar opens.
A Croat woman brings out her accordion.

If men had never gone to sea, who would know?

Athens as Margaret Rutherford

No more
than I care
who I am
here
does she worry
about
what she does
how she looks
or sounds

        When I'm bumped off the sidewalk
        into the street

it's this dame
Margaret
chasing some hussy
tourist
or notorious criminal

        Quoting Oscar Wilde
        or King Arthur or Homer

        she's the heroine
        in whalebone

my bumbling unbalanced godmother
trailing whitewash, loose oranges & lavender
wearing big hats
made out of little Turkish coffee cups

        continually confused
        but never at a loss

for words
or gestures

        seeming

in & around

that touchstone
that construct
that comfort

      that Acropolis of a jaw

always
perfectly
& consistently
alive
fluted
& cylindrical

A Disaster

Some survivors could not yet believe it. Came ashore
clutching bits of cardboard
& useless leather.

Others, who did, blamed the crew, and were anxious
to be interviewed. Those who felt
only lucky
wouldn't talk.

His son hadn't been afraid, a father said.
A cook admitted to praying in the water.

Both captains were alive.
One tried, politely, to explain, but was hushed
by lawyers. The other wept.

Posing for a photograph, "It's an outrage!"
a woman cried. "I'm a bride
from Malta, and all my English trunks
went down.

"There's nothing left—nothing
but my husband."

But cause of the collision
was never established
to anyone's satisfaction.

The Groom's Lament

(After Ch'en Shih-Tao, of whom it was
said: "In order to obtain a good line,
he will shut himself up in a room.")

Now that I've taken a wife,
farewell to those long nights
in the taverns.

No longer lighthearted
with wenches
or sad with friends
beyond sunrise; no longer
sleep cross-eyed in my clothes.

Morning light on the mountain.
Soon I'll have forgotten
how to stagger.
But all this lovemaking!
I'm getting too old for it.

How I Became a Poet

It was between some wars.
I owned a bird called Charles Dickens.
My Lionel electric train was in storage.
And things began to go badly; a friend lost his right hand
& I stopped seeing him. For no reason
hugged my chest. One day fell to the floor selfishly
clutching a sponge.

The bird passed on & I motored to Mexico
speaking sloppy English pretending to be Lindbergh
recognized by thieves & orphans. Lived on Tabasco
& penicillin. Sketched cloudbursts by candlelight
knowing I'd never swim
in Guatemala.

Returned to beloved homeland
to work out dreams. Dead in chemistry
& too late for chess. Boyhood mildewed.
Curious for a week about ancestors. One day woke
fox-footed & dictatorial
issuing meticulous orders for conduct
of the secret life
refusing to carry them out
terrified of heights & snakes.

Read impossible books, got conversational.
Voted, quarreled, registered; punched out my history
every motive questionable. When asked what I was doing
all I could refer to
was what I'd done yesterday. Then fell in love
with sad nights & came to trouble: nothing worse
than being unhappy
in this country. It goes against
the teachings.

But trouble, I found, brought out the best in me.
And poets, I was told, can't be told
how to think, what to feel, or vice versa & have lots
of trouble. So that's what I became. And earlier
when I said "beloved homeland"
that's not what I meant, exactly.
That was yesterday.

Monody for Sheila

Nothing she tried to do for me
ever helped.

When I was home, having trouble
trying to create, she'd arrange herself

as neatly as 11 fresh eggs, & nourish the air
with verbal arabesques.

When away, she sent impressions of me in needlepoint
in various uniforms

obsolete as Spads.

Since the slightest touch of her hand
under any conditions

sent me into deep contemplation
of personal problems

I made love to her savagely
in the shape of an arguing Irishman, or thorn.

Everyone thought we were made for each other.

In the beginning, I was moved by her attentions
because, she said, her one aim in life was to be

graceful, but then I realized
she merely wanted *me* to be graceful.

Not that I loved her less for that, but
as beautiful as she was

left her one day
while she was singing a Bach aria.

It was too bad we couldn't work it out.
The moon has insomnia, she said once. *You can have it.*

"Ramona"

when stars made sense
all songs were moons
& sex was hula dreams
in the high school

> *to tangos i died*
> *a kiss was queens*
> *rabbits were wise*
> *& girls submarines*

fledged my heart
in piracy winks
gypsy surprises in knees
& evening lotions
following dark beautiful
Beatrice, 17

> *to tangos i died*
> *a kiss was queens*
> *rabbits were wise*
> *& girls submarines*

through amber orchestras
gliding suave careers
to violins
& time a croon

o time, a croon
to be lifted like lightning
to love
in arms of a dancing body
& love was till midnight
a tropical land

to tangos i died
a kiss was queens
rabbits were wise
& girls submarines

Nacho Jimenez (Stockton)
vs. Richie Manchaca (Pittsburg) Lightweights
(Kezar Pavilion, San Francisco, Aug. 27, '75)

Neither of you Delta lights
going anywhere. But fast, lean,
furious & fine—all heart
for a tough Six.

No cuts or clinches
effort & concentration intense as lasers
& classic skill—worth more than one line
in anyone's Late Edition.

Close decision. The winner's glove. A quick *abrazo*
& it's over, you disappear in flashy robes
one after the other
up the same aisle.

Break for beer
& then the Main: a couple of Big Berthas
one so scared it's embarrassing
& they stop it
in the second.

Lights out early
in this club
& I'm part of the mob who won't go home
hanging around the dressing room doors
trying to pass as just another eggbeater
waiting to get paid.

You two there
leaning against old bricks in the smoke
almost indistinguishable but aloof & patient
in sharp street clothes
sharing an ancient, awful knowledge

Twin attitudes
of such inviolate repose
I turn away
to see for the first time
like birds at rest
the weary palms
of your small, hotshot hands.

Three Tanka

Sometimes
it gets so bad
I head for the mirror
or just any window
for a nod & wink
from a friendly face

Every time
you walk
up my back
as if
the whole world
suddenly found
the right place to go
for its health

The cat's long sleep
through the party
as if our dreams & laughter
would go on
forever

Some Neighbors to the North

Who retired every night
at nine,
precisely.

And were heard to say,
from time to time
"Bad dog"
only.

I was imagined by the wife
to be a mysterious parcel,
& reported weekly
to the Postmaster.

When the husband came by
he straightened his tie
& forgot why.

Whenever the son
wandered my way
he was swept home
to face the wall.

Later I learned
they'd never owned a dog.
She believed moonlight
caused fevers

And lived in terror
that the boy
might someday
call her by name.

A Neighbor to the South

A civil engineer, is putting up a fence
around his lot.

At other times, I hear him
tap-tapping dramatically
with a little hammer.

Does he suspect my woman has been having dreams
of a liberal nature?
Does he know I hate
liver, tripe, & peppers?

We quarreled just once
over a concrete problem
in my breakfast nook.

But what can be improved by yards & yards
of chicken wire?

The space separating us used to be
a simple cavity. Now it's a series
of countless pentagonal holes.

When I learn to play three marimbas,
that will confuse him—& his wife too, who
gardens in gloves
that go above the elbow.

They'll notify the City Council,
maybe even the police!
Then I'll denounce him
as a collaborator

And throw a dead mouse
perfectly preserved
over his bamboo.

Somebody might get arrested.
Or he may be driven to do the right thing
& return to Oslo
& buy a sailboat.

Oceans Without Tears

On or above oceans
it's a boat, a plane, seaweed, a life raft, birds
or a balloon

Below, it's coral reefs, currents, jellyfish
oil, an old Spanish cannon
or sunken treasure

If you can see only oceans from a certain point
& are not on a ship, or a continent
then you have an island
& I hope you have a radio

If you don't, then all you can do
is look for something safe to drink
find a companion
or build a helicopter

Oceans live among big-breasted harems
of plump winds
with yoga legs & ghostly voices
which can toss & turn you long into the nights

But I like them best
when they're reclining with the stars & the moons
after a good dinner
humming music you can dance to

Your average well-adjusted ocean
sounds like Orson Welles as himself
promoting reasonable wines & mild cigars

You don't have to be an actor, or a sailor.
If you're only a passenger on a submarine
or a castaway
or merely a whale, it's O.K.

More oceans, & driftwood, & icebergs
are what you can always count on
in the end

Three Haiku

Alexander, beautiful
                old cock
you should have won
blue ribbons

My eighth scotch
grandmother how did you
come apart
on that high barstool?

No one home—
   in your garden
      I sit
watching
      butterflies
come
      and go

Resolutions

(After Tu Fu)

Before sunrise I wake
in the bandaged light
of new snow. The city so quiet
it could be mourning the death
of the last whale.

I think of all the best times
glowing like the red & green lights
of disappearing trains.

Across the river to the West
where the moon would be
the whistle of one small boat.
The cats twitch in their sleep
dreaming perhaps of the unborn.

It is early in the year.
I lift my arms, rise on toes
& decide to remain motionless
for three hundred days.